The Peaceful PORCUPINE

by Julie Borowski

Illustrated by
Tetiana Kopytova

This book is dedicated to the peacemakers.

Special thanks to Drew White, Greg Borsch, Darryl Schmitz, Sterling Kellis, Philippe Malzy, Marshall Standifer, Andrew Kaufman, Zachary Zaremba, and Shawn Ansley.

Nappo watched from a distance as the forest animals ran and played together. He wished they would play with him—that he could have just a few friends of his own. But no matter how hard he tried, none of the animals wanted to be friends with a porcupine!

One day, as he was getting a drink of water, Nappo noticed a fly buzzing nearby.
“Hello, fly!” Nappo said. “Would you like to be my friend?”
"No way!" the fly buzzed. "You'll probably wait until I trust you and then come after me with those sharp claws!"

At the fly's words, Nappo grew sad. He would never, *ever* attack someone for no reason. Not even a fly. He was a peace-loving guy!

A few days later as he was climbing a tree, Nappo noticed a squirrel gathering acorns.

"Hello, squirrel!" Nappo said.
"Would you like to be my friend?"
"Heck, no," the squirrel screeched and scurried farther up the tree.
"You probably just want to eat me!"

At the squirrel's words, Nappo was crushed. He would never eat another living creature! He was an herbivore. He only ate plants!

Not long after, Nappo was exploring the woods when he noticed a deer prancing through the trees.

"Hello, deer!" Nappo said. "Would you like to be my friend?"

"Not a chance!" the deer screamed. "You might be smaller than me, but your spikes look like they hurt! Ouch!"

At the deer's words, Nappo felt hopeless. His long, sharp quills were meant to defend him from other animals who wish to do *him* harm. He would never use them to bully other creatures!

"It's no use," Nappo cried. "No one will give me a chance. How will I ever make a friend looking the way that I do?"

A few nights later, Nappo was out searching for food when he heard a whimpering sound. Peering around a bush, he saw a baby rabbit.

"Baby rabbit!" he said. "What are you doing out here without your mama?"

"I'm lost and I can't find her!" cried the baby rabbit.

"It is much too dangerous for you to be out here alone!" Nappo warned the baby. "There are animals in the woods who would eat little rabbits like you!"

At Nappo's words, the bunny began to cry again.

"Oh, don't cry," Nappo said. "It will be okay. I have special ways to scare away predators. I promise, I will keep you safe."

As the bunny drifted off to sleep, Nappo stood guard. He wasn't going to let anything hurt the little rabbit.

The bunny had not been sleeping long when Nappo smelled a raccoon. Displaying his sharp quills, he warned the raccoon not to get any closer.

"I'm out of here!" whimpered the raccoon, and he ran away.

A little while later, Nappo heard a hawk coming from the sky above.
He started chattering his teeth to scare the hawk away.
"I know better than to mess with a porcupine!" the hawk shouted, and he flew away.

Next, Nappo saw a fox sneaking up from behind the bush. He let out a nasty smell to make the fox back off.
"Pee-yew!" the fox said, and he ran away.

"I did it!" Nappo cheered. "I scared away all of the predators! Thanks to me, the little rabbit and I are safe and sound."

In the morning, Nappo heard another rustling in the bushes. He stood ready to protect the bunny, but what peeked through was not a threat. It was the bunny's mother!

"My baby! There you are!" the mama rabbit said. "I've been looking all over for you! Oh, I'm never letting you out of my sight a—"

The mama rabbit stopped short as she caught sight of Nappo. "A porcupine!" she gasped. ”You get away from my baby!”

"Oh, please, don't be alarmed," Nappo said.
"I mean you no harm!"
"But you're a porcupine! Everyone knows you use your spikes to hurt other creatures!" the mama rabbit cried, inching toward her baby.

"No, Mama, it's true! He didn't try to hurt me once," the baby rabbit told her. "In fact, he kept me safe all night long. He scared off a raccoon *and* a hawk *and* a fox!"

"Is that right, porcupine?" the mama rabbit asked Nappo.

"Yes, of course!" Nappo answered. "I would never hurt a little baby. I would never hurt *anyone* unless I had to. My life motto is: don't hurt me and I won't hurt you."

The mama rabbit thought
for a moment.
"That is a very kind
way to live,"
she said at last.

"I'm sorry, porcupine," Mama said. "I was wrong about you. You peacemakers make the world a better place. We could use more of you. Would you like to be our friend?" the mama rabbit asked.

At the mama rabbit's words,
tears of joy came to Nappo's eyes.
"I would love to."

As the sun rose over the forest, Nappo and his new rabbit friends ran and played together. Finally, Nappo had other animals to play with.

"Group hug?" Nappo asked.
"Thanks, but no thanks," the mama rabbit laughed.

Made in the USA
Middletown, DE
14 July 2021

44163542R00018